Original title:
Ferns in the Corner

Copyright © 2025 Creative Arts Management OÜ
All rights reserved.

Author: Seraphina Caldwell
ISBN HARDBACK: 978-1-80581-717-8
ISBN PAPERBACK: 978-1-80581-244-9
ISBN EBOOK: 978-1-80581-717-8

The Gentle Touch of Green Loneliness

In the nook where whispered dreams lie,
A plant stands tall, with a silly sigh.
It sways and dances, a lonesome glee,
Waving at dust bunnies, wild and free.

Its leaves tell jokes that no one gets,
Making friends with old, forgotten pets.
A snicker here, a chuckle there,
Companionship found in leafy air.

Embracing Shadows of Nature's Night

In darkened corners, shadows play,
With laughter echoing night and day.
The leafy forms, a comic troupe,
Throwing shade in a leafy loop.

A jester green, with wiggles so slight,
Tickling the moon in the soft twilight.
Mysterious giggles from beneath the gloom,
In nature's stage, they find their room.

Hidden Life of the Overlooked

What secrets lie in quiet spaces?
In the green, we hide our faces.
The tiny critters, ready to scheme,
Plotting mischief like a wild dream.

With tiny voices, they spin their yarns,
Chasing shadows, finding charms.
A chitter here, a chortle there,
Lively antics fill the air.

Entwined with Nature's Heart

A cozy nook, a world apart,
With ebullient laughs, it's quite the art.
Leaves embrace the sunlight's caress,
In this mingle of joy, who could guess?

Whispers of glee from branches above,
Every twist and turn, a secret love.
In the embrace of each green delight,
Nature's humor sparkles bright.

The Stillness of Green Grace

In the corner they look sly,
With fronds raised up to the sky.
They wiggle and sway with cheer,
Whispers of secrets they hold dear.

A happy dance, a leafy jig,
Growing in chaos, oh so big!
Who knew such laughter from the ground?
In stillness, their joy is found!

Nature's Lurking Curiosity

In a patch so lush and bright,
Green aliens plot by moonlight.
Peeking out from where they hide,
With leafy laughs, they take pride!

Their mission? To steal the show,
While chasing bugs that steal the glow.
What a sight to see them prance,
Nature's quirks do make us dance!

Tangled Whispers in the Gloom

In shadows deep, they spin a tale,
With giggles that make the soft winds wail.
Tangles of green, like hair undone,
Chasing sunlight just for fun.

Each twist a knot of silly glee,
A leafy party, wild and free.
They murmur jokes in the still night,
With raucous whispers, pure delight!

Soft Shadows on the Floor

On the floor, they stretch and sprawl,
Casting shapes that seem to squall.
With shadows that play peek-a-boo,
Creating mischief, much ado!

A playful breeze stirs up the fun,
Tickling leaves just like a pun.
And in those corners, they conspire,
For laughter's the secret they conspire!

Fronds of Solitude

In a cozy nook, they sway with pride,
Awaiting whispers, where secrets hide.
Their vibrant green, a comedic flair,
Tickling dust bunnies, unaware they're there.

Each frond a jester, dancing below,
While the cat ponders, watching the show.
With every breeze, they wave and tease,
Who knew greenery could bring such ease?

Where the Light Meets the Leaves

Sunbeams sneak in, a playful dash,
Leaves giggle softly, in a shimmering splash.
A battle of shadows, a tickling fight,
As sunlight chuckles, kissing them right.

Every glint's a wink, every sway a jest,
Who knew plants could be this blessed?
Dancing in circles, a leafy parade,
In a botanical world where pranks are played.

The Silent Witness of Growth

In stillness they stand, with a grin on their face,
Watching the world, in their leafy embrace.
A riot of nature, no need for a quirk,
As they observe all, from their little perk.

Giggles in green, they're knowing and wise,
Like furry old friends with glittering eyes.
With quips in the shade, they keep spirits high,
As life's little moments drift gently by.

Nature's Gentle Embrace

Cuddled in green, where laughter is found,
Life's simpler joys wrapped snug all around.
Leaves rustle softly, sharing a laugh,
A botanical giggle; it's nature's own path.

In corners tucked away, they love to tease,
The insects that wander, with mischievous ease.
In a world of oddities, they play their part,
Bringing cheer to our lives, straight from the heart.

Secrets of the Hidden Hollow

In the quiet nook, they bide their time,
Dancing shadows with a twist of rhyme.
Secret whispers, giggles in the grass,
Life's little jest in a fleet-footed mass.

Beneath the leafy cloak, mischief blooms,
Caterpillars wear hats, claiming their rooms.
They toast with dew drops, relish the dawn,
While the sun stirs gently, yawning and withdrawn.

Tangled in Nature's Lace

A wild mess of green with a cheeky grin,
Waltzing together, they spin and spin.
A rabbit hops by, tripping on air,
Wondering if there's room for his flair.

Entwined like buddies at a birthday bash,
Leaves play peek-a-boo, creating a splash.
With funny faces, they rock to and fro,
Nature's own jester, stealing the show.

Resilience in the Darkness

In shadows deep where the giggles hide,
Knotted greens with a mischievous stride.
Waves of laughter in the midnight glow,
As stars above cheer on the show.

They thrive in gloom, a secret game,
Tickling the darkness, whispering names.
A beetle's dance, oh what a delight,
Turning the mundane into a light.

The Jewel of the Forgotten Space

Buried treasures in patches unseen,
Blushingly bright, like a vibrant scene.
A squirrel stops short, struck by the view,
Laughing at life in a costume of dew.

In this lovely chaos where giggles grow,
A chorus of crickets joins in the show.
Embracing the odd, the quirky, the fun,
In a world full of laughter, they shine like the sun.

A Tapestry of Leaves and Light

In a nook where sunlight plays,
Leaves dance in their quirky ways,
A chuckle blooms between the fronds,
As nature twirls, its joy responds.

A leaf slips down, it takes a dive,
A rabbit hops, it feels alive,
The breeze teases with gentle shoves,
While sunlight giggles, it simply loves.

Amidst the shadows, whispers thrive,
A bug with swagger, oh so sly,
It struts around, a tiny king,
In leafy realms where laughter springs.

Greenery's charm hides a sly jest,
Nature's canvas, the playful best,
With each rustle, a secret shared,
In joy and mirth, we are ensnared.

The Secret Lives of Shadows

In twilight's hush, shadows conspire,
They stretch and pull, they never tire,
A dance of shades, a funny scene,
Like silly ghosts from a Halloween.

Behind the plants, a giggle waits,
As crickets plot their secret dates,
The sun peeks in, but they all hide,
In their cloaks of dusk, they giggle wide.

A squirrel sneaks in with cheeky glee,
Stirring up chaos, all the glee,
While shadows chuckle, oh so bold,
At antics of creatures, tales unfold.

The nighttime air is full of fun,
With shadows racing, on the run,
Each flicker of light, a prank in stride,
Nature's comedy cannot hide.

In the Embrace of Overlooked Green

In the nook where tiny critters play,
A leafy couch holds secrets sway,
A ladybug in polka dots,
Claims her throne and then just trots.

The daisies giggle, a sassy crew,
While snails parade in their slow view,
Across the floor of emerald bliss,
Each plant, it seems, has a comic twist.

The wind whispers, with a teasing air,
Enticing petals to sway and share,
Laughter spills from every vein,
In the corner, life is quite the gain.

Beneath the guise of simple green,
Lies clownish revelry, unseen,
With every rustle, a jest unfolds,
In this sanctuary, fun never grows old.

Murmurs in the Shade

Under the green, where secrets dwell,
The chatter rises, a rustling swell,
A gnome with mischief, tucked away,
Winks at the sun, oh what a day!

Whispers float from bush to tree,
Laughter hides, just like a bee,
The breeze joins in with a playful spin,
As shadows play and the fun begins.

A sneaky ant in a tiny hat,
Celebrates life with a little chat,
While mushrooms giggle, round and stout,
In the shade, there's never a doubt.

Murmurs echo, in this bright niche,
Each sound a puzzle, a little glitch,
In nature's jests, we find our way,
With warm chuckles in bright array.

In the Stillness of Growth

In the nook where shadows play,
A leafy creature starts to sway.
It dances slow, in quiet glee,
As if the world's just a cup of tea.

Beneath its veil, there's much to find,
Tiny critters, much less refined.
They peek and poke, with winks and grins,
Throwing shade while life begins.

On lazy days, it seems to smirk,
As squirrels bounce with silly quirks.
Unfazed, it watches the antics unfold,
A sage of silence, wise yet bold.

In this haven, life is light,
Where laughter lingers, day and night.
A green companion in the fun,
In stillness, joy weighs a ton.

Shelter Beneath the Green Canopy.

Underneath the leafy dome,
Creatures frolic, find a home.
A snail in shoes just takes its time,
Reciting tales in slow-motion rhyme.

Woeful ants march in a line,
Wrestling crumbs of food divine.
But wait, what's that? A raccoon jive?
A nightly dance to feel alive!

With every rustle, secrets shared,
A parade of chaos, none prepared.
The sunlight chuckles, gleams and bends,
In whispers of green where fun transcends.

So come, lay down your woes and fears,
In this raucous realm of ferns and cheers.
A respite here, from life's own fray,
Where plants hold court and laugh all day.

Whispers from the Green Shadows

In shadows deep, where mysteries lie,
A leafy friend draws nigh to sigh.
"Tell me more!" the shadows plead,
"Of all your mischief, every deed!"

The chatter of leaves in a breezy gale,
A giggling crowd, a leafy tale.
A grasshopper leaps, with flair and style,
While the sunbeams wink with a cheeky smile.

Just when you think, it's peaceful here,
Squirrels plot, and whispers leer.
Stockpiling nuts, they make a fuss,
"With all this green, who needs a bus?"

Among the shadows, laughter reigns,
A comical world of joyous gains.
So heed the rustle, join the fun,
In green shadows, we all are one.

Beneath Canopy Secrets

Beneath the leaves, a secret dance,
Where tiny creatures take their chance.
A ladybug spins, round and round,
While beetles cheer without a sound.

Mischief brews in the leafy brew,
As tiny beings plan their coup.
With every tick, the shadows blend,
Creating tales that never end.

And when the rain starts to descend,
They leap and laugh, their joy won't bend.
A tiny pond fills with delight,
Reflecting chaos, glimmers bright.

So gather close, in this green lair,
Where laughter flutters through the air.
For under cover of leafy shade,
The funniest memories are made.

Whispers of the Shaded Grove

In a nook where shadows play,
The green leaves dance and sway,
A squirrel slips, does a twirl,
Chasing dreams in a leafy whirl.

Beneath the boughs, a game unfolds,
With whispers and giggles, secrets told,
A rabbit hops, trying to hide,
From the antics of the playful tide.

Laughter bubbles like a stream,
With nature's jokes, we all can beam,
A lizard's leap, a slippery glide,
In the grove where chuckles abide.

Breath of earth, a gentle tease,
Here we laugh with crafty ease,
For in the shade, life's never bland,
With humor sprouting, hand in hand.

Lush Secrets Beneath the Canopy

Underneath the leafy veil,
A playful plot begins to sail,
A turtle snores, a frog sings loud,
While fireflies stir and dance proud.

In the dim, where giggles bloom,
A sly fox works on his loom,
Knitting laughs with threads of glee,
For all to share, for all to see.

A whippoorwill tells a tale,
Of a cat whose skip was a fail,
He slipped on dew, made a fuss,
And landed right in a green bus.

With secrets wrapped in leafy dreams,
Laughter bubbles, or so it seems,
In this hangout, life's a jest,
Where joy and nature find their rest.

Shadows of the Frond

In the twilight's easy glance,
Shadows loom, they whirl, they dance,
A raccoon pranks with tiny paws,
Creating mischief without cause.

The whispers here play tricks on ears,
As rustling leaves bring funny cheers,
A beetle slides, a snail takes flight,
In shades where humor takes its bite.

Laughter springs from every nook,
Across the ground, a wild book,
Where tales of giggles intertwine,
In leafy laughter, all's divine.

A frog declares his croaks as tunes,
While fireflies join as little moons,
Together they weave a festive night,
In the corners where joy ignites.

Verdant Escape in Quiet Nooks

In emerald realms where whispers drift,
A squirrel's leap provides a lift,
He stumbles once and makes a face,
As laughter echoes through the space.

In a quiet spot to unwind,
Nature's jokes are unconfined,
A snail, so slow, claims to run,
But charms all with a smile and pun.

A raccoon's hat is flipped askew,
He tiptoes softly: 'What's new?
Just gathering snacks for a feast,'
While mischief lingers, to say the least.

As moonlight spills on leaves so bright,
The hidden jokes take flight at night,
In every nook, a giggle springs,
In nature's heart, the laughter sings.

The Quiet Burden of Ephemeral Life

In the shadows where laughter blooms,
Green leaves wiggle, dodging brooms.
They giggle and whisper tales of old,
A secret life, a sight to behold.

Tickling dust and hiding shy,
Like introverts under the sky.
Each rustle a jest, a quiet snicker,
Life's fleeting dance, oh, how it flickers.

In corners where sunlight barely creeps,
They stand stoutly, their vigil keeps.
Yet whispers of humor are lost in their sighs,
As they wonder where the mischief flies.

With a wave of the hand, they flip their fronds,
As if in jest, they simply respond.
Life is short, they nod with glee,
In their stillness, a laugh so free.

Gentle Spirals of Something More

A winding dance in shades of green,
They sway and curl, a comical scene.
Twisting like pretzels, they tease the light,
Each spiral a giggle, pure delight.

Who needs a tale of grandeur or might?
These leafy curls hold joy outright.
They plot and plan a leafy parade,
With whispers of mischief, decisions made.

Intertwined secrets of the forest floor,
With stories of humor and laughter galore.
In every frond, a chuckle lies deep,
As they cuddle the shadows, in silence they keep.

A ribbon of green with a cheeky stance,
They lure you in for a frolicsome dance.
In corners where no one seems to roam,
They craft a world that feels like home.

Verdant Echoes in the Stillness

In the hush where laughter does stow,
Silhouettes sway, a verdant show.
As silence reigns with a playful wink,
These green pranksters make you think.

An air of mischief, slight and sweet,
They nod and chuckle, their leafy feat.
Each flicker of light, a tease from the back,
Whispering secrets on a playful track.

Layers of green in a quiet parade,
With every curl, a joke is made.
A leafy comedy, booming and bright,
In stillness, they revel in pure delight.

As shadows stretch and days grow long,
They sing in silence their own silly song.
Nature's jesters, bold and spry,
In their universe, the giggles fly.

Shadows Softly Drifting by

Whispers of green in the dusk's embrace,
Soft shadows flick to a joyful pace.
In a quiet corner, a kindred spirit,
Fronds shake with laughter, can you hear it?

Tiptoeing softly on a breeze so light,
Adventures unfold in the depth of night.
Each swish and sway, a secret affair,
Mischief and whimsy float in the air.

Cheeky curls nod like friends in jest,
Trading small stories, all in a fest.
With every turn, a giggle spills,
In the quiet corner, life gives us thrills.

As shadows gather and twilight calls,
They wear the humor like leafy shawls.
In the stillness, the laughter runs high,
Life's whimsical dance gently drifts by.

Where Shadows Breathe Green

In a nook where laughter grows,
A plant plays peek-a-boo with toes.
It tickles thoughts of summer's past,
And claims the best of shadows cast.

A dancer sways in merry glee,
While clumsy pets trip joyfully.
It whispers jokes to passing flies,
And giggles softly 'neath the skies.

Among the muted hues it spins,
Caught in a dance where fun begins.
Though lost in light, it plans to scheme,
A secret life, a playful dream.

With every wiggle, every sway,
It conjures tricks to brighten day.
A leafy friend with cheeky charm,
That offers hugs and won't alarm.

Veiled Whispers of the Whispering Ferns

Beneath the shade, a giggle hides,
With leafy arms, it gently glides.
It whispers tales of garden woes,
And tickles toes where no one goes.

In corners dark, it spins its threads,
Of playful pranks and nightly spreads.
A frolic far from glancing eyes,
With laughter dressed in green disguise.

When morning light breaks through the gloom,
It stretches wide and fills the room.
Sharing secrets with the breeze,
Despite its shyness, it aims to please.

Those veils of green, they twirl and flap,
Around the stones, they form a trap.
To catch the smiles as they dart by,
Creating joy that can't say why.

The Hidden Life of Lush Green

In a shady spot, mischief brews,
With creatures sneaking playful snooze.
A tiny leaf, a cheeky grin,
Hides a world that spins within.

Joking roots that twist with flair,
And tickle bugs that linger there.
Each frond a jester, sprightly, bold,
Guarding secrets, stories told.

When sunbeams nestle, laughter swells,
With silly sounds that no one tells.
A chorus made of rustling cheer,
That whispers softly for all to hear.

With every sway, a giggly tease,
It spins a fanciful unease.
Yet under growth so rich and bright,
It charms the day into the night.

Unraveling Solitude in Green

In solitary spots, laughs abound,
Where shyly nestled life is found.
A mix of velvet, slyly spry,
It chuckles low as folks pass by.

Perched on the edge of friendless walls,
It entertains the drumming calls.
With every shadow that it casts,
It fears the future, but stays steadfast.

With nature's jokes as its best mates,
It talks of love in leafy states.
A riot dressed in vibrant hues,
Transforms the mundane into clues.

Alone, but never truly so,
It pulls the curtain, puts on a show.
To strangers passing, gives a nod,
A merry sign from nature's squad.

Secrets of the Shaded Sanctuary

In the nook where the shadows play,
Mossy gossip keeps worries at bay.
Silly whispers from ferns so sly,
'They swear that the foxes wear ties!'

Looming leaves in laughter do sway,
As squirrels jive in their own ballet.
The daisies giggle, puffing their cheeks,
As hedgehogs boast of their secret techniques.

A rabbit grins, his ears like a fan,
He tells a tale of a brave man.
When night falls, they'll dance in a line,
While crickets chirp a rhythm divine.

So secrets lie in the shady glade,
Where nature's circus is marvelously made.
Join the jesters in their frolic and fun,
In a world where the giggling won't shun!

Tucked Away in Nature's Fold

In the heart of the woods, where secrets reside,
A family of squirrels throws parties with pride.
Branches shaking with each little cheer,
'Who needs the sun? We've got cold root beer!'

Beneath rustling leaves, the rabbits convene,
Playing leapfrog in their grassy green sheen.
They wager on which one can jump the farthest,
As the wise old owl gives a hoot that's heartiest.

Dancing shadows, the mushrooms can't wait,
Forming conga lines, oh isn't it great!
With a twist and a turn in syncopated cheer,
Even the rocks are tapping, oh dear!

Tucked away in this laughter-filled realm,
Nature's silliness takes over the helm.
So tiptoe softly, step in with glee,
There's a party tonight, just you wait and see!

Verdant Hues of Tranquility

In the green paradise where giggles thrive,
The mushrooms declare they're professionally alive.
They paint their caps with colors so bright,
Stirring up mirth in the soft, leafy light.

The bushes chime in with their rustling lore,
'There's a snail who's racing! Just wait, there's more!'
With a crowd on the sidelines, they count every move,
'If he wins, I swear we'll all have to groove!'

A parrot swoops down, with a voice loud and clear,
'Smell the fresh air? It smells like good cheer!'
Leaves start to shimmy, swaying with zest,
Making a dance that nature finds best.

So let's raise a toast to this riotous scene,
To verdant vibrance that's lively and keen.
Take in the humor, the joy in the leaves,
For laughter in the wild never deceives!

A Whisper Amongst the Greens

In the gentle breeze where the funny winds blow,
The trees hold secrets we're dying to know.
They whisper to flowers with petals so bright,
'Watch out for the ants; they're planning a flight!'

Underneath tangled vines, a turtle does scheme,
Dreaming of racing, oh isn't he keen!
Yet, stuck in his shell, he can only retreat,
While frogs leap around him, oh isn't that sweet!

A chuckle erupts from the grasses so fine,
As the ladybugs lead a parade in a line.
With tiny little trumpets, they march and they play,
'This grass is our stage—what a glorious day!'

So lean into laughter and breathe in the cheer,
The greens hold a humor that's so very dear.
In the wild, let giggles be your guiding song,
For in nature's embrace, it's here you belong!

The Secret Garden's Breath

Whispers of green in a dusty nook,
A plant's conspiracy, come take a look.
Leaves chuckle softly, tickle the air,
Who knew they'd plot, with such flair?

With each little sprout and curious bend,
They tease the squirrel, and prank the friend.
A dance of shadows, a game of peek,
Secrets of growth, at their shadiest peak.

Oh, the gossip that circulates here,
Of bugs and sun, and plenty of cheer.
They trade all the tales of a summer fling,
While the daisies roll eyes, and the lilies sing!

In their verdant realm, chaos ensues,
As nature's comedians spread their news.
A ticklish breeze, just for fun's sake,
In this playful patch, all jokes awake!

Ribbons of Verdure

Beneath the floorboards, a green surprise,
Wiggling and jiggling as sunlight complies.
They wear coats of emerald, quite the rave,
Life's little party, in shadows they wave.

A spotted leaf waves like a goofy friend,
Mocking the weeds that dare to offend.
They twist and they twirl as if in a race,
Adding a punchline to nature's embrace.

In the silence of rooms, their laughter flows,
With roots like old tales that nobody knows.
A flutter of life, as they hold court,
Guardians of humor, in nature's retort.

So let's not forget those who grow with glee,
The cheeky green sprites, the vibrant esprit.
May their jokes be plenty, their antics chic,
Ribbons of life, in the nook so unique!

Elegance Amongst the Neglected

In a corner forgotten, sat quite a sight,
A lady in green, in her gown of light.
With ruffled edges, she sips the sun,
"Who needs a garden? I have all the fun!"

Dust bunnies whisper, "What's this all about?"
"Oh dear," she chuckles, "Do you have a doubt?
While you lounge in the grime, I'm bringing the class,
With style and with grace, I'll give you a pass!"

Beneath the old shelf, her laughter composes,
Together with shadows, and time's little doses.
Chasing the stillness, they waltz through the air,
A comedy troupe with a flair so rare.

In elegance hidden, they tease and delight,
Making the mundane ignite with their light.
So here's to the shy ones, with laughter to share,
Witty and wise, in their cozy lair!

The Quiet Dance of Green Life

The silence quivers, a tickle unplanned,
As leafy folks gather, all hand in hand.
No grand stages here, just floorboards and smiles,
Little dancers prance, as nature beguiles.

A gentle sway, with a pinch of whim,
As shadows play games on a twilight whim.
"Who needs the spotlight? We've got our own tune,
Let's jig and let jive, beneath the bright moon!"

With whispers of cunning, and giggles so sweet,
They rustle for rhythms, and dance on their feet.
Their rustling grass skirts, a comical sight,
They boogie till dawn, in the cloak of the night.

So here's to the buds with their grand soirée,
In the corners of life, they dance and they play.
A boastful parade, with a chuckle and cheer,
In quiet corners, their laughter is clear!

Testaments of Time in Stillness

In shady spots they dance with glee,
Whispering secrets, just wait and see.
They laugh at clocks, it's quite a show,
As shadows stretch and sunlight flows.

A mystery wrapped in green delight,
They even giggle at birds in flight.
With each new sprout, a jolly cheer,
Oh, to be green, with nothing to fear!

Time's a joke in their leafy reign,
While we rush on in life's fast lane.
They quietly snicker, with roots that know,
Life's best moments often move slow.

So when you pass, just stop for fun,
Join the green crowd—you're not done!
Laughter lingers where life is free,
In their stillness, we find our glee.

Patterns Unfolding in Soft Light

Sunlight dances on tender greens,
Crafting stories in playful scenes.
Leaves uncoil with a silly twist,
In nature's quilt, none can resist.

They stretch and wave like jolly fans,
Making shapes in fanciful plans.
The light reveals what shadows hide,
Their quirky poses, they're filled with pride!

Swaying softly, they toss their heads,
Chasing dreams where humor treads.
Each shadow flicks a gentle tease,
Nature's gossip on a playful breeze.

In the morning glow, watch them beckon,
Time to frolic in the light they reckon.
With every sigh, they drift and sway,
Patterns of joy come out to play.

The Silence Between the Leaves

In summer's hush, they have a chat,
Of beetles, bugs, and the occasional cat.
A pause in the stir, they whisper low,
About the world and its crazy flow.

Each leaf a speaker, with tales to weave,
Of mischief made when no one believes.
A squirrel who stole a shiny ring,
And the funny things that birds can sing.

As twilight falls, their voices blend,
The laughter hums, a timeless trend.
And though they stand, quite still and meek,
In whispered tones, they're far from weak!

Amidst the quiet, let humor thrive,
For every leaf is truly alive.
In silence thick, their jokes take flight,
A leafy chorus, what pure delight!

Memories of Mossy Embraces

A cushion soft, like hugs from trees,
Where critters scamper, enjoying the breeze.
Mossy beds that cradle the tales,
Of woodland tricks and scent of trails.

A ticklish touch beneath our toes,
Nature's carpet where laughter flows.
Creaking logs wear emerald coats,
Each step a giggle, as joy promotes!

Here lies a toad, with a wink so sly,
While old roots sigh a jovial why.
The memories shared in the damp embrace,
Bring silly grins to each wandering face.

As twilight wraps in a gentle fold,
Living soft tales, both new and old.
In every nook where softness stays,
Laughter echoes in mossy ways.

The Corner's Silent Wisdom

In a nook where whispers blend,
Silent green speaks to a friend.
Hints of laughter brush the air,
With leafy jokes that none would share.

Dust motes dance in sunlit beams,
Nature's watchman, there it seems.
It chuckles softly, plays it cool,
The wise old plant, the corner's fool.

Roots entwined with tales untold,
Old and new in silence bold.
With each new sprout, a jest anew,
In the shaded spot where secrets brew.

Yet mischief lurks with playful grace,
Stirring the shadows in their place.
Knotty fibers weave a dream,
In corners where the sunlight gleams.

Shadows and Light in Unison

Underneath the bright delight,
A dance of shade takes flight.
Foliage sways, a soft ballet,
While chuckles echo, come what may.

The sun smiles down, so full of cheer,
While green giggles hiding near.
In that patch of leafy fun,
The mischief has just begun.

Beneath the leaves, a secret tease,
Whispers carried on the breeze.
Nature's jesters in disguise,
With leafy limbs and longing sighs.

They plot to tickle dust from skies,
Chase shadows where the laughter lies.
In this corner, joy's reprieve,
A silly tale we all believe.

The Story Beneath the Surface

Beneath the green, where giggles hide,
A tale is spun, by roots supplied.
With whispers low and secrets sly,
In this patch, the stories fly.

A sandy bed, so soft and sweet,
Cradles antics, paved with heat.
Tiny worlds both old and young,
With twirling tales left unsung.

Creeping vines play tricks at dusk,
Tickling feet with leafy musk.
In every frond, a wink, a grin,
A woodland plot designed to win.

The laughter rises, soft and clear,
In the soft earth, it's drawing near.
And in the quiet, joy springs forth,
From twists and turns, of nature's worth.

A Retreat into Green Silence

In a cozy spot, under the spray,
Where secrets roam and shadows play.
The greens conspire, sly and sly,
Telling jokes that make you sigh.

Each leaf a story, funny and grand,
Of silly things that light up the land.
Bursts of laughter, soft as mist,
In a muted harmony, none resist.

So come, sit down, embrace the cheer,
In this verdant nook, have no fear.
With rustling tales and mirrored grins,
The green brigade knows where fun begins.

In silent whispers, they convene,
In this emerald corner, a happy scene.
The world outside fades away,
Leaving giggles to rule the day.

Secrets Under the Leafy Canopy

In shadows deep, where whispers creep,
A spider's dance, a secret's leap.
Tiny creatures, oh what a show,
Under the green, they come and go.

The leaves above, a gossiping crew,
Spilling tales of the morning dew.
A raccoon giggling at a nearby snail,
While birds chime in, with a comical tale.

Laughter rises with a rustling sound,
As ants march boldly on the ground.
Nature's humor wrapped in green,
Where silly antics reign supreme!

So peek beneath, and you may just see,
The wild laughter of a whimsical spree.
In the leafy world where dreams unfold,
Secrets dance in shades of bold.

Nature's Whispering Comrades

Amidst the green, let's take a glance,
Where critters gather for a prance.
A squirrel spins tales of daring feats,
While the toad croaks out funny beats.

Chirps and chortles, the air is bright,
As owls swap jokes in the soft moonlight.
Grasshoppers leap with humorous flair,
In this wild jesting, there's laughter to share.

A hedgehog snickers at a passing breeze,
While butterflies dance with utmost ease.
The thickets echo with joy and cheer,
As nature's pals whisper, "Come join here!"

In this communion, joy takes its stance,
A merry melody, a grand romance.
So lean in close, listen and grin,
For laughter in nature's where fun begins!

An Undertone of Verdancy

In soft green hues, the mischief brews,
Nature's jesters wear leafy shoes.
A prankster beetle on a sunlit leaf,
Jokes with the shadows, a comic thief.

Frogs in tuxedos croak with style,
Each jump and splash brings a warm smile.
Even the flowers nod their heads,
As they gossip 'bout the snails in beds.

The rustle of grass, a chuckle so sweet,
As critters share secrets on tiny feet.
A wandering breeze toys with the presents,
Dancing through greens, the humor's effervescent.

In vibrant hues, the antics delight,
Under the boughs, day turns to night.
So pause a while, join in the spree,
In this playful world, we twirl carefree!

The Embrace of the Shaded Realm

Beneath the boughs, where the coolness plays,
Laughter echoes through shaded bays.
A raccoon wearing a sun hat wide,
Sips from puddles, oh what a ride!

Mice tell tales with a cheeky grin,
Of the cat who tried but never wins.
The ferns giggle as the wind sways,
Joining in on sunny, jovial days.

A curious fox with a twinkle bright,
Winks at the moon, oh what a sight!
The shadows chuckle with every turn,
In this merry nook, for joy, we yearn.

So here beneath the foliage spread,
Join in the laughter, no cause for dread.
In nature's embrace, find delight so grand,
For every creature now takes a stand!

Lush Thoughts in Forgotten Spaces

In a pot that's seen better days,
A green cloud dances and sways.
It whispers jokes in the light,
As dust bunnies giggle in flight.

A leaf unfolds with a grin,
Snickering at where it's been.
A shadow plot thickens near,
Where sunlight and nonsense volunteer.

Who knew that a tiny sprout,
Could hold humor through a drought?
It tickles roots with a pun,
Making hard times feel like fun.

In quiet corners, laughter grows,
Among the weeds, a chuckle flows.
Each twist and turn in the breeze,
Keeps spirits high with perfect ease.

Curled Leaves of Memory

A twist of green, a shade of cheer,
Reminding us the past is near.
Each curl, a secret, a tale,
Of sunlit paths and winds that wail.

With every rustle, a story unfolds,
Of frolics in meadows of gold.
The laughter echoes through the air,
As shadows dance without a care.

Memories tucked in each little fold,
Giggling at ages, both young and old.
In the laughter of leaves, we find,
A whimsical world that's well-designed.

When the breeze tickles their sides,
They burst out laughing, between the rides.
In the playful whispers, we get our fill,
Of nostalgia swaying with every thrill.

Nature's Quiet Embrace

In nooks where the sunlight plays,
Nature's charm takes a humorous gaze.
A chortle from the branches high,
As leaves map out their own sly lie.

With a gentle rustle so stealth,
Green gatherings boast of hidden wealth.
Each shadow a laugh, with secrets keen,
In a wild green world that's seldom seen.

Proclaiming joy in every hue,
Life's funny in this leafy view.
Buds tease their neighbors, all in fun,
In the wisdom of green, the jokes are spun.

A cozy blanket of colorful cheer,
Wraps around hopes and shenanigans here.
In the embrace of nature's grace,
Laughter lingers in every space.

The Shade of Resilience

Beneath the broad green canopy,
Lies a party of roots, oh so zany!
They tickle the earth, tease the dirt,
While blossoms giggle in their shirt.

A laugh breaks free from the stillness,
Reminding us of life's true silliness.
In the quirky curves and bends,
The humor of nature never ends.

With a wink, the leaves declare,
Life's a joke worth the wear and tear.
They stand tall, with a playful strife,
Finding joy in the cracks of life.

In shadows cast by laughter bright,
A resilient heart shines in the night.
These jests from nature bring delight,
Rendering the mundane, out of sight.

Muffled Secrets in a Darkened Space

In shadows thick where whispers creep,
A gathering of greens takes a peep.
They chuckle soft, with leaves so light,
As if they're plotting fun all night.

A spider weaves its tale so sly,
While beetles dance, they leap and fly.
Who knew in this dark little room,
Nature's laughter might just bloom?

A gnome rests with a smirk so wide,
As mossy friends come out to bide.
With twigs as hats, they play their part,
In this leafy realm, they steal your heart.

So tiptoe past, don't make a sound,
In secret corners, joy is found.
Though silent, the greens have much to say,
In this quiet place where they play!

A Dance of Leaves in Stillness

Amidst the breeze, a jig does start,
With leaves in pairs, each leaf a heart.
They twirl and spin without a care,
In leafy skirts, they float in air.

A playful robin joins the fun,
Chasing shadows, all in the sun.
While mice on tiptoes prance along,
They join the symphony, oh so strong!

With acorns clapping, a beat so sweet,
Nature's dance with tiny feet.
A concert held beneath the sky,
Where even whispers manage to fly.

So gaze upon this grand display,
Where greenery laughs the day away.
A frolic shown in a simple glance,
Tomorrow's tales will surely enhance!

Quiet Tales from the Green Realm

In stillness held, where shadows play,
The greens conspire in their own way.
A tale of moss that's grown with glee,
Whispers of worlds that you can't see.

The ladybug, a wee detective,
Unravels truths so quite selective.
With every crawl, a story spins,
Of secret gardens and tiny wins.

Sunbeams poke through, the giggles soar,
As beetle bands start up the roar.
In grassy courts, they play their parts,
And share their dreams with all their hearts.

So sit awhile, let laughter flow,
Among the greens where wonders grow.
Each leaf a chapter, every sigh,
An epic tale beneath the sky!

Life Waiting in the Gloaming

As daylight wanes and shadows creep,
Life stirs in corners, secrets keep.
With fireflies blinking, a winking show,
Night unfolds, the magic glows.

A hedgehog hums a tune so bright,
While crickets croon to greet the night.
Amongst the greens where laughter lingers,
Fingers of stealthy breeze touch all fingers.

The blooms stay shy, with petals curled,
As giggles float through twilight's world.
They tease the sun to stay a while,
With every flutter, a secret smile.

So wander through this veiled delight,
Where shadows dance and ease the fright.
In gloaming's hush, life takes a chance,
To whisper secrets and softly prance!

The Unseen Beauty of Quiet Corners

In shadows where the dust bunnies play,
A leaf whispers secrets in a decorum ballet.
Tiny critters hold a grand masquerade,
While cozy earth cradles the jokes that they've made.

A spider winks with a mischievous grin,
As acorns declare, 'Let the laughter begin!'
Sunlight escapes through the dust motes afloat,
Playing peek-a-boo in a sunbeam coat.

A rogue mushroom will curry some fame,
With jokes about toadstools; they're all quite the same.
While the old wooden bench nods off in mirth,
Dreams doubly forgotten, for all that it's worth.

So, salute to the corners where humor will thrive,
With whimsy and green, these spaces come alive.
For laughter's the moss that can cover a stone,
In the unseen beauty of a place all its own.

Secrets Nestled in Nature's Arms

Once in a corner where two paths collide,
A squirrel spills tales that squirrels confide.
Blades of grass giggle, they dance in the breeze,
While snails gossip slowly, with utmost of ease.

An old tree's wise knots seem to keep in a plot,
Of secrets and murmurs, oh what have they got?
The stones wear their moss like a green velvet cloak,
While shadows chuckle with each little poke.

A dandelion dreams of far-off delight,
While crickets compose their tunes late at night.
Laughter's a language that all can discern,
In that hidden embrace of nature's grand turn.

So come take a peek where the secrets reside,
And join in the jest with the beauty that's wide.
For every lost tale finds a friend in the charms,
Nestled away in nature's warm arms.

The Understory of Forgotten Dreams

Beneath the tall giants where shadows unite,
Whispering dreams that have taken to flight.
Mice in their jackets tell stories in haste,
Of cheese heists and mishaps, the thrill of the chase.

A wandering gnome chuckles under the ferns,
His cap tipped just right, oh the way that he turns.
With jests about footwear mismatched in bliss,
And how every dreamer can't resist seeking this.

Robins with quips sing songs that disarm,
While ivy entwines with its usual charm.
The underbrush hiding a raucous good time,
Where laughter erupts without reason or rhyme.

So never forget the wild whispers in shade,
For the dreams that once were, a new path they've laid.
Each chuckle, a treasure where wishes get spun,
In the understory laughter outshines the sun.

Lattice of Shadow and Sun

In a patch where the sunlight and laughter entwine,
A petunia's antics are quite hard to define.
Dandelions frolic with daisies at play,
As shadows throw parties when bright turns to gray.

A sunflower snickers with pollen-filled pride,
While the bushes gossip and giggle beside.
"Did you hear about last night?" they whisper in jest,
"Where the moonlight blushed, and nightingales dressed!"

The lattice of light makes designs on the ground,
As though nature's humor knows no bounds.
With every rustle and tickle in air,
The corners of gardens will always declare.

A chorus of chuckles and whirs fills the deep,
In this patch of delight, where laughter won't sleep.
So revel in moments the sun chose to run,
Through the lattice of shadows, where joy's never done.

In the Cradle of Green Shadows

In a pot of leafy laughter,
Whispers of a plant brigade,
Hiding secrets, silly banter,
Underneath the sunlight's shade.

Jokes about the bugs that crawl,
Dancing in a wobbly sway,
Flipping fronds, they have a ball,
Leaves have more fun every day!

Like a green and leafy choir,
They strut in their fashion show,
Each one prouder, even higher,
Swaying to a breezy flow.

Charming quirks in every leaf,
Chuckles echo 'neath their shade,
Nature's jokers, beyond belief,
Poking fun in every glade.

A Sanctuary of Whispers

In a dance of leafy schemes,
A gathering of giggles blends,
Chatting softly in their dreams,
Nature's jesters, playful friends.

With a flick and gentle twist,
They wave at shadows passing by,
Mischief blooms, you can't resist,
As they flirt with breezes nigh.

Oh, the tales they softly weave,
Of the sunshine and the rain,
In their sanctuary, they believe,
That every drop's a punchline gain.

Tickled by the rustling air,
They snicker at their leafy fate,
Guardians of humor, laid bare,
Laughter's sweetest green escape.

The Unsung Guardians of Calm

Hanging loose in sunlit spaces,
With a smirk, they soak the glow,
Whispering in leafy traces,
Secret jokes that only they know.

In the stillness, they conspire,
Brazenly with nature's flair,
Making mischief, they conspire,
Rustling giggles fill the air.

Satire blooms in every frond,
With roots that tease the ground below,
Stealthy humor, magic wand,
Turning stillness into show.

They stand sentry, all in green,
Watching life with joyful glee,
Masters of the unseen scene,
Plant comedians, wild and free.

Green Veils in Stillness

Veils of green don't take a break,
Chuckle softly as they sway,
Twisting like a cheeky bake,
At the world's absurd ballet.

With family roots all intertwined,
They gossip in the sunshine's glow,
Plotting pranks, a leafy kind,
At the garden's lively show.

In secret thickets, they confide,
Fluffs of laughter gently roll,
Comic relief wrapped up in pride,
In their leafy, tranquil stroll.

Their humor grows beneath the light,
Absurdity the written law,
Guardians of joy, pure delight,
In their garden—laughter's draw.

Shadows of the Verdant Realm

In a nook where light is shy,
Leaves dance with a gentle sigh.
They wave to the dust, say hi,
As visitors pass, they just comply.

Twisting and turning in the shade,
Mocking the sun, a grand parade.
Sipping on whispers, so unafraid,
Of prying eyes or plans they've made.

Little green sentries, standing tall,
Watching the world, at their leafy mall.
Giggles of shadows, in a leafy hall,
Waiting for someone to drop a ball.

In this realm where silliness reigns,
An audience of roots, all in chains.
What happens here, stays without stains,
Just antics of plants and their whimsical games.

The Subtle Art of Being Overlooked

In the background, they play their part,
With a cunning smile—who'd have thought?
Beneath the duster, they make art,
Whispers of laughter that can't be caught.

They catch your eye, yet you look away,
Waving their fronds in a quirky display.
"Notice us please!" they silently sway,
In the game of hide and seek, they play.

Each petal a puppet, and it's all a show,
A comedy sketch that grows and grows.
With tricks up their leaves, what a dazzling glow,
Who knew being green could steal the dough?

They paint the room with whimsy and cheer,
While humans complain, "Where's the beer?"
But little do they know, in their sphere,
Life is just a joke, oh dear, oh dear!

In the Embrace of Leafy Guardians

Cuddled up in their cushy spot,
Guardians of giggles, plot after plot.
With vines and tendrils, a lively knot,
They scheme and dream of mischief, a lot.

In their green capes, they wiggle and sway,
Each leaf is a sidekick, ready to play.
When guests walk by, they'll shout, "Hooray!"
To brighten the mood, in a jolly way.

A tangle of humor on breakfast tables,
Telling stories that warp and fables.
With a wink from a frond, they craft their labels,
"The best-kept secrets, as long as they're able!"

As sunlight spills through their leafy embrace,
A chorus of chuckles fills the space.
For in their realm, it's a curious place,
Where silly adventures dance with grace!

Green Intrigue in a Sunny Room

In a sunbeam's warmth, they stealthily joke,
A leafy assembly with tons of poke.
They peek at the humans, partake in the smoke,
Of laughter and chatter, all day they stoke.

These loopy green pals, so sprightly and spry,
With long, leafy limbs that reach for the sky.
They whisper sweet truths that might make you cry,
Yet chuckles abound as they covertly fly.

They claim the best spots, slight of hand,
While humans ignore, as if it were planned.
A twist here and there—oh how grand!
Just waiting for someone to take a stand!

So when you glance over, give them a cheer,
For through all the foliage, mischief is near.
A meeting of laughs, their mission so clear,
To lighten the burdens that humans hold dear.

The Life Behind the Lattice

Behind the slats, a dance unfolds,
A secret party nobody holds.
Each leaf a guest wearing a grin,
Whispering stories of where they've been.

The sun sneaks in through gaps of space,
Illuminating their leafy embrace.
Caterpillars cha-cha with laughter bright,
While spiders spin dreams until the night.

With every breeze, a giggle escapes,
An adventure wrapped in green capes.
They plot and scheme in their leafy retreat,
As the world outside bears heavy feet.

So peek through cracks, see their delight,
In the lattice shadows, it feels just right.
Join their revelry, no need to refrain,
In the dance of the leaves, joy shall remain.

Green Heartbeats in Still Spaces

In the quiet nook where dust bunnies thrive,
Green heartbeats pulse, keeping dreams alive.
A whimsical waltz with no one to see,
These leafy performers, what could they be?

One leaf tilts sideways, a wave of hello,
While another rolls laughter with the flow.
They argue and banter like siblings at play,
Daring the sunlight to join every day.

Beneath the shelves, they've made a delight,
Coloring shadows with shades so bright.
A light-hearted buzz fills the air around,
In the stillness, joy and mischief abound.

So tiptoe softly, in silence, be sly,
To catch the shenanigans where wonders lie.
With each heartbeat, they wriggle and sway,
In their little kingdom, forever they'll stay.

Ferns of Forgotten Tales

Once upon a time in a dusty old crate,
Lived leaves with secrets, all waiting for fate.
They whisper old stories, and giggle with glee,
Of dragons and fairies from age's marquee.

Each frond spins a yarn in the hush of the room,
Of treasure maps hidden and impending doom.
While moss eavesdrops with a knowing smile,
And the shadows chuckle, staying awhile.

In their leafy library of laughter and dreams,
Each tale, like daylight, bursts at the seams.
Forgotten yet vivid, they dance on a whim,
A theatrical show that's delightfully dim.

So come, gather 'round, as the stories unfold,
In the realm of the green, where legends are told.
Who knew that old leaves could bring such delight?
With a flick and a twist, they brighten the night.

A Haven of Green in the Dust

In a cluttered corner where creatures reside,
A haven of green plays the host with pride.
Tiny bugs picnic on leaf-bustled shores,
With grasshoppers crooning and dancing galore.

Dust motes waltz through the sun's warm embrace,
While the greens wiggle and bumble in grace.
No room for boredom, they quirkily chat,
While napkin-clad ladybugs swirl like a mat.

They speak of adventures on winds soft and kind,
Of gardens and jungles, of trails left behind.
Though days may be still, the laughter persists,
In the heart of their haven, it's joy that exists.

So lift the old box, reveal their delight,
In a world made of green, where spirits take flight.
With each little petal, a giggle is found,
In a charming old corner, pure magic abounds.

Unseen Murmurs of the Foliage

In corners where whispers dance and sway,
Lurking leafy gossip shows the way.
A cheeky plant with secrets to share,
Eavesdrops on chatter from the sunlit air.

The soil holds tales of mischief discreet,
Like garden cads with tiny green feet.
They wiggle and giggle, a leafy delight,
While curious rabbits peek out at night.

A bumblebee's buzz, a scolding lark,
Provide the soundtrack for green's little arc.
Whistles and chuckles in leafy disguise,
Underneath branches where humor lies.

So next time you stroll by that shady spot,
Remember the laughter, the tales that are hot.
Nature's own stand-up, with antics galore,
Echoing joy from each leaf, evermore.

Nature's Soliloquy in Green

A leaf tells a story with an upside-down grin,
Boasting of raindrops that tickled its skin.
It sways to the rhythm of the soft, gentle breeze,
While critters giggle 'neath the watching trees.

A dandelion ponders, with a fluffy head,
Of the silly designs that the wind overtread.
With each silly tumble, it cracks up with glee,
As squirrels roll 'round in their mad jubilee.

Through twisted stems where hilarity stirs,
A chorus of chuckles in nature prefers.
Chirps and croaks join in, a cacophony bright,
In this comedic stage, all under moonlight.

So listen intently, don't rush on ahead,
Nature's own jokes are quite easily spread.
As each playful plant sings and it frolics around,
In green's theatre of laughter, joy abounds.

Hidden Stories Beneath the Canopy

Under the arch where the shadows convene,
Sneaky whispers of humor weave through the green.
A shy mushroom giggles, its cap all askew,
While a snail's slow dance gets applause from the dew.

The ancients of earth, like chortling trees,
Share the most hilarious of secrets with ease.
A worm wears a wig made of dirt and delight,
As ladybugs chuckle, their spots shining bright.

Thickets conspire in winks and in grins,
While shadows join in where the laughter begins.
With beetles in bowties and ants in a line,
This cozy cabaret makes the trees intertwine.

So linger a moment, don't hurry your chase,
For nature's convolution is a whimsical place.
With each hidden tale, a smile will appear,
In the shade of the foliage, laughter is near.

The Enchantment of Shadows Cast

In the shade of the boughs where the silliness thrives,
Shadows are throwing the best of their jives.
A cheeky old twig taps its tiny cane,
While the sun plays peek-a-boo, trying to gain.

The laughter entwined, like a tickly vine,
Pulls everyone close, the mood's so divine.
A bushy-tailed rascal, with antics so bold,
Steals berries away, while the laughter unfolds.

The roots share their secrets in soft, hushed tones,
As critters play hopscotch on smooth river stones.
While night softly whispers, it joins in the fun,
Shooting stars giggle, twinkling on the run.

So look to the shadows, they spark with delight,
Where silliness blooms in the cool of the night.
Nature's own carnival, a stage made of light,
Awaits in the corners, so cozy and bright.

Echoes of a Leafy Heart

In the corner, greenery sits,
Winking at my daily bits.
With a shimmy and a shake,
They tease me for my mistakes.

Their laughter fills the sunny space,
As I trip over my shoelace.
They whisper secrets to the chair,
While I pretend not to care.

Underneath their leafy guise,
They chuckle at my silly sighs.
I serve them tea in tiny cups,
And they giggle as it spills up.

They sway like dancers in a trance,
Tempting me to join their dance.
While I sip and sip and sip,
They remind me not to slip.

Green Sentinels of Solitude

In the shadows, guardians grin,
Making sure the fun won't thin.
They nudge me with a leafy sprout,
Saying, 'Come on, let's check it out!'

With no plans I sit all day,
But green friends have a better way.
They twirl around and jump in glee,
Encouraging my clumsiness spree.

I trip on my thoughts, make a mess,
As they nod to my clumsy stress.
These quiet jesters never tire,
Reminding me to find my fire.

Each rustle, each playful breeze,
Whispers, 'Hey, life's meant to tease!'
And in their quiet, leafy fun,
I realize I'm never done.

Ferns of the Hidden Nook

In the dim light of a hidden space,
Green wonders chuckle at my face.
They wiggle in pots, so full of charm,
While I stumble, trying not to harm.

Their leafy fingers beckon me close,
Like old pals boasting a hilarious dose.
They tell tales of the dust and grime,
Of travels too wild, oh what a time!

When I spill my snacks, they cheer and glance,
Hoping for crumbs in a leafy dance.
With each bite, they nod, they sigh,
Supporting my munching with a leaf-happy cry.

They often remind me with their glee,
That life's a fest if you lean on me.
With jokes aplenty, under the light,
These leafy jesters make everything bright.

Life in the Forgotten Cradle

Amidst the dust, old tales unfold,
In this nook, laughter is bold.
Life hums softly, hidden in green,
Where secrets abound, unseen, unseen!

They peek from corners, giggling low,
As I wander in, unaware of the show.
With a sprout here and a vine there,
They throw laughter into the air.

If I dare to take a seat,
They scoff, oh what a simple feat!
With jests and jives, they chuckle near,
Reminding me to shed my fear.

In each whisper of rustling fronds,
I find a solace that responds.
And as sunlight dances through the space,
I embrace the joy of their leafy grace.

The Green Tapestry in Stillness

In corners where shadows blend,
Lies a dance that won't quite end.
Whispers tickle the timid air,
As the leaves plot a secret affair.

Lurking low in a gentle stand,
With a wave, they make their demand.
"Join us here, come take a peek,
We've got mischief we're bound to speak!"

Sunlight giggles through the gloom,
As they lounge in relaxed bloom.
Each frond with a quirky pose,
Giggles spark, as nature knows.

And if you stop and take a seat,
You might find laughter in their beat.
For in their still and leafy pride,
Lives a jest that they can't hide.

Echoes of Nature's Embrace

In the hush where green things chat,
A riddle sings from where they sat.
Soft crickets join the leafy jest,
With a thrum that never takes a rest.

A chorus sways in cool delight,
As shadows jiggle with their height.
"Come closer, we're safe!" they tease,
With a sway that aims to please.

Underneath the sun's sly grin,
Adventures whisper, where to begin?
Amid the laughter, leaves confess,
They're the kings of low-key mess.

With every breeze, they start to dance,
Inviting all for a goofy glance.
Nature's jokers, sprightly crew,
Crafting giggles in every hue.

Hidden Flora in Soft Light

Beneath the gaze of sleepy beams,
Shy bushes plot their leafy schemes.
Unseen laughter fills the air,
In frilly robes, they pause and stare.

While sunlight tickles their green tips,
They chuckle quietly, no need for quips.
"Did you hear the one about the stone?
It claimed it could never be outgrown!"

Soft shadows flicker on the wall,
In this giggling woodland hall.
With every rustle, you'll find a clue,
That nature's jokes are all too true.

So tiptoe close and take a look,
At the plant life's secret book.
Amongst the shades, the chortles rise,
As mischief dances in disguise.

Ferns of Serenity

In the nooks where lizards lounge,
A leafy troupe begins to scrounge.
"Who's the best at hide-and-seek?
Let's challenge them, it's all unique!"

They spread in whispers, bold and bright,
In every crack, there's joy in sight.
With textures fuzzy, colors green,
Nature's roguish, leafy scene.

Underneath the sun's warming rays,
They amuse with their clueless ways.
"Watch me dazzle, watch me sway,
At being silly, come what may!"

And if you feel the urge to join,
Just follow where the fun's in coin.
For in the calm, they thrive and play,
With laughter brightening each new day.

www.ingramcontent.com/pod-product-compliance
Lightning Source LLC
Chambersburg PA
CBHW052221090526
44585CB00015BA/1409